Familiar Spirits, Witchcraft and Satanism

Innocent Beginnings, Deadly Results

by
Dr. Hilton Sutton

HARRISON HOUSE
Tulsa, Oklahoma

6th Printing
Over 48,000 in Print

Familiar Spirits, Witchcraft and Satanism —
Innocent Beginnings, Deadly Results
ISBN 0-89274-667-X
Copyright © 1989 by Hilton Sutton
Mission To America
736 Wilson Road
Humble, Texas 77338

Published by Harrison House, Inc.
P.O. Box 35035
Tulsa, Oklahoma 74153

Contents

Introduction   9

1   How It All Began   13

2   Witchcraft — An Abomination To God   17

3   Astrology Is Idolatry   23

4   Deadly Results   27

5   What Are Familiar Spirits?   33

6   Bible Examples of Familiar Spirits   47

7   "Dabbling" in the Occult   55

8   Satanism: A Rampaging Obsession   69

9   Witchcraft and Familiar Spirits —
What You Can Do About It   83

Bibliography

A Note From the Publisher:

Dr. Sutton's research of Satanism; obtained from law enforcement agencies in Texas, New York, New Mexico and California; revealed violent acts performed by Satanists. The accounts in this book describe some of those acts. After careful consideration, we — author and publisher — decided to include those descriptions in order for the Body of Christ to be alerted to the extremes of Satanism.

Introduction

Originally when I began speaking and writing on the subject of familiar spirits, witchcraft and Satanism, people would often ask the question: Why do you speak and write on this subject?

The answer I gave was that God has assigned me the work of interpreting the prophetic Scriptures and placing the events of our present day alongside the prophesied events.

But today, my purpose is to alert the reader to the dangers involved in the occult. Since I published my first book on the subject of witchcraft and familiar spirits, there has become a wider acceptance of this evil, satanic force. Also witchcraft and other occult activities have grown in epidemic proportions.

Journalists in the fields of television, newspapers and magazines have given this demonic subject prime-time exposure. Numerous Hollywood actors and actresses have announced their involvement, especially with astrology and reincarnation.

Several women mediums now appear publicly and, for a price, allow an audience to observe them as they permit a demon spirit to take them over on stage.

One such person declares that an ancient 35,000-year-old wizard possesses her. She then speaks with a strange voice to her audience with so-called wisdom and philosophy of the ages.

The world seeks for signs, and the desire for insight into the future is ever-increasing. Satan is certainly aware of carnal desires and attempts to satisfy them. However, He is a deceiver at work to kill, steal and destroy. (John 10:10.)

With so many people already involved in some form of witchcraft, it has become a major problem in the world. I have written this book for the benefit of all whom Satan would attempt to entrap in this subtle, sophisticated, and sometimes intelligent-sounding operation.

The Apostle Peter informs us that our adversary is the devil and that he desires to devour us. (1 Pet. 5:8.)

Well, I've got bad news for the devil: A born-again, Biblically informed Christian can and will put him to the sword — the sword of God's Word! We will not be taken in by his craftiness, but we will show him some fine swordsmanship which he can't handle.

Even though it may seem as though there is no solution to this serious problem, remember we have *the solution — Jesus Christ,* and He has given us authority in Him to use His Name and His Word against the power of Satan.

Greater is He that is in us, than He that is in the world. (1 John 4:4.) Satan is our defeated foe and God has equipped us to keep him defeated. We are more than conquerors through Jesus Christ. (Rom. 8:37.)

...ye shall know the truth, and the truth shall make you free.

John 8:32

1

How It All Began

All of us are members of a generation with problems as great or greater than at any previous time. Over the last two or three decades, we have been observing an explosion of witchcraft and drugs that is unequaled in our society.

How did it all start?

The decade of the fifties was a time in which America became caught up with the intellect. School campuses filled with students, and it was the "in thing" to be an intellectual. However, many of the educators by that time had become either agnostic or outright atheistic. The mind was exalted above God.

What part of the human being does Satan desire to control? Of course, it is the mind. Therefore, mind control is his goal.

From the fifties came the saying, "We don't know who we are, and we don't know where we're going." People were crying out that they were lost, but the Church really didn't hear their cry. It was tragic! The intellect without godly influence is an easy takeover for Satan.

The intellectual fifties exploded into the rebellious sixties. The sixties became the decade of protest, demonstrations, and riots. Every form of constituted law and order faced resistance. The home, the family, marriage, authority at school, discipline at work, the government, even the Church — all took a beating.

The decade of the sixties was indeed a dark, difficult, and horrible time in America. One word clearly summed up the mood of the country: rebellion.

In First Samuel 15:23 God told King Saul of Israel:

> **Rebellion is as the sin of witchcraft, and stubbornness is as iniquity and idolatry. Because thou hast rejected the word of the Lord, he hath also rejected thee from being king.**

Saul's problem was simple: he chose not to obey God. He sought the services of a spiritualist medium, and the ultimate outcome was death. (More about the tragic story later.)

Rebellion against God creates an atmosphere in which Satan can begin his most subtle, most sophisticated, and most devastating work! As we will learn in this study, he begins by slowly involving a person with a familiar spirit; then he captivates his mind, causing an addiction to witchcraft and in many cases even mind-altering drugs. He must gain control of the mind.

God declared that rebellion would result in witchcraft, and it certainly has. Today witchcraft has combined with a drug usage in this country that has grown to major proportions. God does know what He's talking about!

Witchcraft and drugs are not new. History records their use among most pagan tribes, where Satan had a stronghold, where he was worshipped.

Today these two very satanic operations are often used by sinister, satanic mediums and gurus to deceive people into believing that witchcraft or drugs are a way to God. But God cannot be found through either of them!

Jesus declared, . . . **I am the way, the truth, and the life: no man cometh unto the Father, but by me** (John 14:6). God has never been found through the use of witchcraft and drugs. Only through Christ Jesus can He be found. Only through Christ Jesus can a person come to know God on a personal basis.

How cunning Satan is in this hour. The Apostle Paul, in writing to the church at Corinth, warned how Satan himself could be transformed into an angel of light. (2 Cor. 11:14.) He also described how Satan's ministers transform themselves into ministers of righteousness.

Why?

To deceive those who do not know the Word of God nor the Lord Jesus Christ. Such people can be misled and taken captive by a "pseudo-spiritualism," which in the truest sense is witchcraft in its most devastating form.

Revelation 9:21 reads: **Neither repented they of their murders, nor of their sorceries, nor of their fornication, nor of their thefts.**

This verse of scripture describes the exact situation that will exist in the last three and one half years of the Tribulation Period as men on earth fall into four distinct categories of godlessness: murderers, sorcerers, fornicators, and thieves.

It isn't as though these categories of wickedness, violence, and corruption were not already evident. We certainly can see the effect of them today; in fact, they are on the increase. But one of these categories is of particular interest to us in this study: sorcerers.

In most Biblical references, when the word sorcery is used, it carries the singular interpretation: witchcraft or enchantments. However, when used in the book of Revelation, the word sorcery has a different root and carries the definition: witchcraft involving drugs.

Ours is definitely the generation in which this sinister operation has begun. This is not to say we are already in the Tribulation Period; but we are in the prelude, the forerunning days.

As Biblical prophecies are being fulfilled, bringing the world nearer to the Tribulation, one must know that all the systems and vehicles to be used by Satan would have to be in operation prior to that seven-year period.

What began in the decade of the sixties is an announcement that the Tribulation Period must be rapidly approaching.

There are many scriptures throughout the Word of God that warn against witchcraft. They cover the many facets of witchcraft prevailing now across the United States and around the world.

In this study we will cover quite a number of them. It is important that you examine the Scriptures for yourself to see what they have to say about witchcraft and familiar spirits.

2
Witchcraft —
An Abomination To God

In Deuteronomy, chapter 18, we find God's instructions to His people regarding some forms of witchcraft. Let's read verses 10-13:

> **There shall not be found among you any one that maketh his son or daughter to pass through the fire, or that useth divination, or an observer of times, or an enchanter, or a witch,**
>
> **Or a charmer, or a consulter with familiar spirits, or a wizard, or a necromancer.**
>
> **For all that do these things are an abomination unto the Lord: and because of the abominations the Lord thy God doth drive them out from before thee.**
>
> **Thou shalt be perfect with the Lord thy God.**

These instructions of God are simple. He states that there should not be found among His people any of those who fall in the categories mentioned, and He doesn't miss a single evil classification.

The first classification of witchcraft has to do with using fire as a test of purity — making a child walk on or through fire to fulfill some religious activity. This act is broad enough to include even human sacrifice.

Some may think that human sacrifice is a thing of the past, but authorities report that such activities occur today in many large American cities. The sacrifice of children still goes on in India and other pagan countries. Several years ago, the remains of human beings were discovered in an abandoned munitions dump near Houston, Texas. Authorities later revealed that several adults had been sacrificed during witchcraft activities in which drugs were used.

Law enforcement authorities tell us that they believe human sacrifice and, in particular, child sacrifice is now widespread throughout the world. No one would ever believe it could happen here in the United States, but it has and it is!

These authorities tell us that many children who have disappeared have become a human sacrifice for some group who either worship Satan or some other false god. Satan worship, although nothing new, is now spreading throughout America like wildfire. It must be stopped!

The second category mentioned in Deuteronomy 18 is divination, or possession by a familiar spirit. Acts 16:16 tells of a young woman who used divination. The original Greek calls it *the spirit of a python*. She possessed the satanic ability to charm her victims until she and the spirit possessing her could take control of their minds.

An *observer of times* strongly implies an astrologer. The prophet Isaiah nails astrology to the wall in chapter 47, verses 12-14. There he pointedly states that there can come no good counsel or advice from an astrologer, since the astrologer cannot even save himself.

An *enchanter* is a medium who possesses the evil ability to cast a spell over another person. The black magic and voodoo of Africa, Latin America, and parts of the southern United States is widely known. It involves rites, fetishes, and various charms.

Witches, wizards and warlocks are still very much in operation. There are organized groups in the United States as well as in England, and their involvement usually covers the whole spectrum of witchcraft.

A *charmer* is one who uses words and/or trinkets to bring either good or bad luck to a person.

A *consulter with familiar spirits* describes a medium at a seance. The term *necromancer* also falls into this category. A necromancer is a medium who attempts to communicate with the dead. Such was the act attempted by the witch of Endor at the request of King Saul. (1 Sam. 28:7,8.)

These activities are forbidden by God. They are an abomination to Him.

Everyone must decide for himself whether or not he believes what God has declared. God did not stutter. Neither are His statements left for the interpreter to decide what He meant to say.

There is no way a true believer, or born-again Christian, can participate in any of these activities. For one to call himself a Christian and practice any form of witchcraft would be an act of rank disobedience.

God has declared all these forms of witchcraft to be an abomination to Him; and He further shows them to be imperfect. Satan never does anything right; even his most cunning operation can be discovered and defeated.

Since God has declared this satanic operation to be imperfect, they who trust in these things are always left "holding the bag." They never get a correct report. Satan always covers his lies with more lies.

Further on in the 18th chapter of Deuteronomy, we read these words in verses 20-22:

> But the prophet, which shall presume to speak a word in my name, which I have not commanded him to speak, or that shall speak in the name of other gods, even that prophet shall die.
>
> And if thou say in thine heart, How shall we know the word which the Lord hath not spoken?
>
> When a prophet speaketh in the name of the Lord, if the thing follow not, nor come to pass, that is the thing which the Lord hath not spoken, but the prophet hath spoken it presumptuously: thou shalt not be afraid of him.

Is it not amazing that God's Word covers every false operation, even utterances from false prophets?

Today many are prophesying falsely. God says that if it does not come to pass, it did not proceed from Him.

People use the name of God to propagate their false doctrines among His people; then they attempt to strip away our ability to check them out.

It is so easy to accept a person's claim that his or her gift or word has proceeded from God. When one foolishly accepts such a statement and does not check it out according to the Word, he immediately opens himself to be preyed upon. Sooner or later it happens: another person is swallowed up.

Check out everything! Prove all things! Try every spirit and determine if it be of God. You must do so. The Apostle Paul wrote, . . . **He that is spiritual judgeth all things** (1 Cor. 2:15).

Of course, the truest test is to wait and see whether or not that which is spoken comes to pass.

In 2 Thessalonians 2:3, the Apostle Paul wrote, **Let no man deceive you by any means.**

Not by their mystical spirituality, personality, pulpit ability, oratory, reputation, nor the crowd among whom they are numbered on their popularity. Deception is Satan's tool by which he works to gain mind control.

Satan is very cunning in his moves to capture the mind. He works overtime with the power of suggestion, attempting to start a chain reaction of events, in which people literally help manufacture fulfillments.

Satan speaks or prophesies outright lies that are designed to sound like the truth. Then he uses these lies in such a way that the victim gets caught and actually aids the satanic plan. Once the victim begins to believe the lie, he is soon in Satan's clutches.

3

Astrology Is Idolatry

Almost everyone is aware that the Scriptures speak strongly against idolatry. Idol worship was a practice of the heathen who had no god; therefore, he worshipped many things. Among the pagan gods were the sun, the moon, and the stars. Planets have long been the favorites of fallen man when it comes to choosing idols.

Things haven't changed much in nearly 6,000 years! In fact, more people today have made idols out of the planets than ever before as the result of a pseudoscience called astrology.

Deuteronomy 4:19 has this to say about it:

> ...And lest thou lift up thine eyes unto heaven, and when thou seest the sun, and the moon, and the stars, even all the host of heaven, shouldest be driven to worship them, and serve them, which the Lord thy God hath divided unto all nations under the whole heaven.

There can be no question that this verse is referring to astrology. In the 4th chapter of Deuteronomy God was warning Israel against idolatry.

Astrology claims to foretell the future by studying the position of the sun, moon, and stars.

This is absolutely forbidden within the Scriptures. The sun, moon, stars, and other planets are not to be worshipped. Yet there are those who have literally set up altars to them.

Many Americans rise early every morning and read their newspapers, checking out their horoscope, getting daily advice as to whether or not the day will be good or bad. Anyone who depends upon astrology and his "horriblescope" (Yes, your read correctly, I said "horriblescope"!) for direction and guidance in his life is depending upon one of the most shrewd and deceptive maneuvers of Satan.

It is easy to see how astrology can lead to such dependence on the planets that it soon becomes a form of idolatry.

People quickly deny that they are worshipping the stars, but they just can't wait to get their latest astrological forecast. They are quick to read what some famous clairvoyant or astrologer has to say about their future. All this material is based on the effect that the sun, moon, and stars supposedly have on human affairs. The interest is particularly focused on the sign of the zodiac associated with one's birth date.

Not too many years ago, only a few people knew anything about astrology and the signs of the zodiac. This group was limited to fortunetellers, astrologers, mediums, and their followers. The average person shied away from such an involvement.

Today astrology is so popular that mediums are a dime a dozen. Magazines are filled with this mind pollution and sold by the millions. Signs of the zodiac can be seen everywhere.

Let me make the comment here: Within the history of true Christianity, there is absolutely no record whatever of the signs of the zodiac or the study of the planets.

Because true followers of Jesus study the Bible, they know that astrology is witchcraft. All of these things are the shrewd maneuverings of evil spirits and doctrines of devils designed to deceive people — to capture their minds, bring them into the possession of familiar spirits, and eventually take them into the torments of hell.

Let us consider yet another statement by God. In the book of Exodus, chapter 20, we read verses 1-6:

> And God spake all these words, saying, I am the Lord thy God, which have brought thee out of the land of Egypt, out of the house of bondage.
>
> Thou shalt have no other gods before me.
>
> Thou shalt not make unto thee any graven image, or any likeness of any thing that is in heaven above (planets and stars), or that is in the earth beneath, or that is in the water under the earth:
>
> Thou shalt not bow down thyself to them, nor serve them: for I the Lord thy God am a jealous God, visiting the iniquity of the fathers upon the children unto the third and fourth generation of them that hate me.
>
> And shewing mercy unto thousands of them that love me, and keep my commandments.

God is so kind and concerned about everyone that He sets forth multitudes of warnings. We all learn by repetition, and this is the method God is using on this subject.

God puts His instructions in simple terms, saying, "Don't have any other gods but Me. Don't worship anything that is in the heavens, on the earth, or in the waters." Again, you can easily see that astrology is the worship of the sun, moon, and stars.

Other references within the Scriptures emphasize that it is forbidden to worship the heavenly host. References to the heavenly host do not refer to God the Father, God the Son, or God the Holy Ghost, but to the other planets of this galaxy.

Because man was created by God, he has an innate need to worship. If a person doesn't worship the one true God, then he will find something else to worship.

4
Deadly Results

One Biblical account that clearly shows the effect witchcraft can have is found in Second Kings, chapter 21. It tells of Manasseh, one of Israel's kings, who was a spiritualist practitioner. All information leads us to believe that Manasseh was a high priest of witchcraft.

Verse 3 reveals that Manasseh worshipped the heavenly bodies and built temples unto them — something his father Hezekiah had destroyed during his reign. Verse 3 says:

> **For he built up again the high places which Hezekiah his father had destroyed; and he reared up altars for Baal, and made a grove, as did Ahab king of Israel; and worshipped all the host of heaven, and served them.**

In verse 5 we read how he even went so far as to build altars **for all the host of heaven in the two courts of the house of the Lord.** Manasseh had become so vile and haughty that he actually built ungodly altars right in the house of God! Not only did this violate the Holy Scriptures, but it brought defilement to the house of worship.

Verse 6 says:

> **And he made his son pass through the fire, and observed times, and used enchantments, and dealt with familiar spirits and wizards: he wrought much wickedness in the sight of the Lord, to provoke him to anger.**

Manasseh became increasingly wicked. Not only did he eventually destroy himself, he brought much suffering to Israel and Jerusalem. His spiritualist activities provoked God to anger.

It is difficult to believe that anyone would ever want to provoke God to anger. However, it is very evident from the Scriptures that the pursuance of witchcraft in any form will set that person on the brink of serious trouble with God.

Consider the full destructive forces of witchcraft:

First, it is a hideous tool of Satan, designed to destroy.

Second, the person involved has begun the slow process of suicide.

Third, it brings on trouble with God.

No wonder God is slow to anger, long-suffering, and patient with people. Otherwise, no one would be saved. Thank God for His loving-kindness!

Today people testify about the help and advice they are receiving from astrology and other forms of witchcraft. Could this be true? Absolutely not!

Bible truth to back me up is found in Isaiah 47:12-14. I referred to this passage previously in the book, but now let's take time to read it. Verse 12 says:

> **Stand now with thine enchantments, and with the
> multitude of thy sorceries, wherein thou hast laboured
> from thy youth; if so be thou shalt be able to profit,
> if so be thou mayest prevail.**

Isaiah is saying, "Let's see you operate in all your enchantments and witchcraft. Then we'll find out if you're going to profit by them and prevail in life."

Observing America today, we see more and more people involved with the occult — a hidden, mysterious designation of certain mystic arts such as various and sundry forms of witchcraft, magic, clairvoyance, and astrology.

The same group suffers from extreme nervous disorders, as well as all kinds of emotional and mental problems. Psychiatrists have their hands full trying to help these distressed people.

Occasionally, help is received through psychiatry; but, remember, a psychiatrist cannot rid a person of demonic influence or control. Only God has the answers that will help the spirit-oppressed and possessed.

It is no wonder that the rate of suicide and drug addiction is so high among the emotionally disturbed. Witchcraft is an operation that the devil has designed to totally destroy you — spirit, soul, and body.

Now let's consider verse 13 of Isaiah 47: **Thou art wearied in the multitude of thy counsels.**

There are many kinds of mediums. People involved with fortunetellers, clairvoyants, and astrologers are very fickle. While following a particular medium, they appear very loyal; but let a new medium arise, and some quick changes occur. People are always looking for something better, never satisfied with what they have. After all, they say, the new medium may possess some mystical powers not known to the others!

Isaiah's statement is so true: . . . **wearied in the multitude of thy counsels.**

Let me firmly state that when we know Jesus as Savior and Lord, we have discovered the best. No improvements can be made. Our relationship with Jesus only improves as we continue our daily walk with Him.

The generation we know today has been a searching one — tossed from pillar to post, left in confusion. As an example, let me share an incident that occurred in one of our seminars.

Several young men who were involved in an Eastern religious cult attended the meeting, but they really didn't come because they wished to learn anything. At the end of the session they stood and said:

"We want to invite you to one of our meetings. One of the apostles of the great 15-year-old guru from India is going to be speaking. We'd like for you to come and really hear the truth and get insight to the light."

Satan has numerous followers who are passing themselves off as ministers of righteousness. How the devil likes to come as an angel of light! He gets considerable mileage out of his ability to appear in that way. (Read carefully 2 Cor. 11:14,15.)

I responded to the young men with these words: "What you are involved in is an Eastern occult religion that has been around for thousands of years. If it worked in the areas of the world from which the gurus come, then certainly those areas would be virtual paradises today. Instead they are the most destitute areas in the world."

I called their attention to the statement of Jesus from John 14:6 in which He said, . . . **I am the way**.

Their attitude was: "We knew you would be intolerant and unwilling to accept anything other than the teachings of Jesus."

They admitted knowing about Jesus and said they accepted Him; however, their acceptance put Him in the category of a guru, not as Savior and Lord. They were deceived into believing that their teenage guru from India was the "master of divine light."

As Isaiah 47:13 says, **Thou art wearied in the multitude of thy counsels.** In other words, "So you've sought out many different wizards for advice and a glimpse into the future."

He continues: **Let now the astrologers, the stargazers, the monthly prognosticators, stand up, and save thee from these things that shall come upon thee.**

Isaiah gets very personal and names astrologers, stargazers, and monthly prognosticators. (That takes in all the present-day witches and wizards.) He is saying, "Let's see if there is really any salvation for spirit, mind, and body in all of these things. Let them save you if they can."

Do you think such things can save you? Well, they can't! Here's the reason in verses 14 and 15:

> **Behold, they shall be as stubble; the fire shall burn them; they shall not deliver themselves from the power of the flame: there shall not be a coal to warm at, nor fire to sit before it.**
>
> **Thus shall they be unto thee with whom thou hast laboured, even thy merchants, from thy youth: they shall wander every one to his quarter; none shall save thee.**

Isaiah simply makes it very plain: None of these people can offer anyone good advice or predict the future. The only thing they can do is deceive you into acting on their power of suggestion, eventually getting you to carry out their evil plan.

5

What Are Familiar Spirits?

God's plan calls for ministry to the righteous by His angels. In Psalm 91, the Lord spoke through the pen of David. In verses 11 and 12 he says:

He shall give his angels charge over thee, to keep thee in all thy ways.

They shall bear thee up in their hands, lest thou dash thy foot against a stone.

From this scripture and others comes the doctrine of guardian angels. In Hebrews, chapter 1, the Apostle Paul states that angels are ministering spirits sent to the heirs of salvation. He clearly declares that the ministry of angels is for us and in our behalf.

Because Satan always attempts when possible to counterfeit or copy God's plan, he also uses his fallen angels to carry out his program. Among these fallen angels (or demons, as they are generally called) we find a category referred to as familiar spirits.

The word *familiar* is derived basically from the same Latin word used for *family* and is applied to that which is known through constant association, usually with reference to persons. The association of devils with people is clearly established by the Scriptures.

Satan assigns one of his familiar spirits to an individual or family. The basic purpose of such an assignment is to determine whether or not a particular party is susceptible to spiritual things. If so, then there begins the process of collecting a very intimate and detailed file of information on that party. (Such an assignment is usually made on only one person and rarely on an entire family.)

In understanding how these familiar spirits operate, it is important that you know a few elementary things about these spirits, or demons. Demonic activity is designed to harass, agitate, vex, overpower, and eventually possess a person.

A familiar spirit on assignment does not take possession of his victim. He operates in the spirit world as would an intimate servant in behalf of his employer. He possesses many supernatural abilities and all are used for deceptive purposes, never constructively.

Since he has the advantage of carrying out his mission in the invisible spirit world, a familiar spirit can remain undetected by any natural means.

Acting in his hidden role, he can observe his victim night and day, at work and play, alone and accompanied, and be able to learn the most intimate details of that person's life.

Within his file he collects all kinds of information: talents, resources, friends, neighbors, enemies, likes, dislikes, habits, mental abilities, educational abilities, and responses to many different situations. It is the responsibility of the familiar spirit to put everything he can into that file. He literally must get to know that person from A to Z.

Over a given time period, he learns exactly how his victim will respond to many kinds of circumstances and stimuli. He can actually determine patterns of thought by using the power of suggestion.

Let me firmly declare at this point that Satan and his demons cannot read your mind. Only God knows your thoughts. (See Matt. 9:4, 12:25; Heb. 4:12.) Satan can only guess about what you are thinking, based on his awareness of your lifestyle and your previous response to power-of-suggestion stimuli.

Once a familiar spirit has learned the "in's and out's" of a person and completed his file of information, his assignment changes. He then begins to maneuver that individual into the presence of a spiritualist medium.

Spiritualist mediums fall into several categories. Not all mediums conduct seances in which an attempt is made to communicate with the dead. They also include fortunetellers, astrologers, magicians, sorcerers, clairvoyants, and so on. Their "talents" vary, but all have one thing in common: All are possessed by familiar spirits and their operations are very strongly forbidden by the authority of God's Word.

A medium is a person who has become literally taken over, and or possessed, by a familiar spirit. All spiritualist mediums, regardless of their category, are demonized. I cannot emphasize strongly enough this fact: Fortunetellers, clairvoyants, astrologers, seance mediums, reincarnationists — all are demonized!

Once the familiar spirit has successfully maneuvered his victim into the presence of a spiritualist medium, he is ready for the next step. He very simply transfers the file of detailed information he has created on that person to the familiar spirit that possessed the medium.

The transfer of information occurs through use of the spiritual law of transmitting and receiving. One spirit has no trouble communicating with another in the spirit world.

We are aware of the law of transmission through study of the Scriptures. The Apostle Paul teaches from First Corinthians 12:9,10 how this law is put into operation by Holy Spirit-anointed believers. Among the nine gifts of the Spirit given to the Church, which Paul lists in this Scripture reference, are the gifts of the word of wisdom, the word of knowledge, and discerning of spirits.

Paul lets us know that the Holy Spirit can impart divine information. This then places the believer at an advantage over Satan and his wiles.

However, since God can transmit information to His angels and to His children through the law of transmitting and receiving, Satan can do the same. A familiar spirit has no difficulty sharing his information with another spirit.

When a person is brought into the presence of a medium, the familiar spirit living in and controlling the medium receives the file of information that was collected by the familiar spirit assigned to that person. The medium, in turn, receives that information from his familiar spirit and uses it to "read" his new customer.

The information revealed through the medium includes very intimate details of that person which no one else could know. The customer is hooked! He thinks, "I've never seen this person before. How could he (or she) have known so much about me?"

The medium and the controlling spirit will use only as much information as is necessary to captivate the individual customer, and a second visit is arranged.

At the second meeting, even more such information is revealed, bringing the victim further into the trap. Once the person has returned, the trap is shut with an announcement by the medium that his or her ability is god given. Such an announcement is designed to completely disarm the victim.

From that point, the person is drawn into a very deep and destructive series of events which can eventually lead to his becoming possessed by a demon. The spiritualist medium will tell of things no one else knows or could possibly know.

How did the medium come by this information? Through the transfer of information between the demon spirits.

Reincarnation

The operation of familiar spirits thoroughly explains the inner workings of reincarnation and seances in which attempts are made to communicate with the dead. (More about this later.)

The doctrine of devils known as reincarnation is actually the work of familiar spirits which possess people and cause them to believe they have lived a previous life.

It is not much of a problem for familiar spirits to convince people of reincarnation. There are numerous reports of people who say they have lived in some previous time and place. They relate details of events that took place at that time, and often these facts can be authenticated.

One of the most outstanding accounts of supposed reincarnation was the Bridey Murphy case that occurred some years ago. A number of leading American magazines carried the story which many considered to be a major psychic breakthrough.

Bridey Murphy was a woman who underwent psychiatric analysis. Through hypnosis she described events and details that apparently belonged to a previous life. When her story was checked out, many of the details she described were found to be authentic. The psychiatric profession was greatly impressed.

I have spoken with psychiatrists who have used this method of hypnosis to probe into a person's mind. The stories they relate are amazing; yet all are the work of demons. Satan has very little trouble outwitting the intellectual, carnal mind.

Remember, familiar spirits have been existing since the archangel Lucifer fell from heaven and took a third of the heavenly host with him. Lucifer became Satan, the devil; and his angelic followers became the demons of hell.

For thousands of years these evil spirits have been possessing men and women. It is no problem whatsoever for a spirit to implant in one person's mind certain information regarding a previous life of someone he had possessed.

The Bridey Murphy story gave a big boost to the teachings of reincarnation, which is built upon a concept of steps of perfection. If in the present form of existence a person passes all the necessary tests, he will return in a higher state in his next life. Each step will take him closer to perfection. According to the reincarnationists, after that person successfully passes the tests of numerous periods of existence in various life forms, he will graduate to a state of eternal bliss.

At its best, the doctrine of reincarnation involves people with devils, particularly familiar spirits. The Bible cannot, and will not, support such an evil, cunning, and intellectual doctrine. In fact, the basic teaching of reincarnation is literally contrary to the teachings of the New Testament.

In the 4th chapter of Ephesians, the Apostle Paul makes very clear that the saints are perfected by the ministry gifts to the Church — apostles, prophets, evangelists, pastors, and teachers. The process of spiritual growth and development called perfection is not achieved by steps of reincarnation, but by the supernatural, God-given ministry of the Lord Jesus Christ handed down to the Church.

This life-giving ministry is continued by the Church, particularly through the ministry of gifts which God set in the Church for the perfecting of the saints.

Nowhere in the Word of God is there teaching to support a returning to another life after death and continuing the process until reaching perfection. The

Bible firmly states in Hebrews 9:27, **And as it is appointed unto men once to die, but after this the judgment.**

Some reincarnationists, in an attempt to Biblically support their doctrine, use certain statements from the Bible about John the Baptist. They claim that John was the prophet Elijah returned from the dead. If one carefully reads the account in the Gospel of John, chapter 1, verses 19-23, he will discover that it is impossible to use this Bible record to prove John the Baptist was Elijah reincarnated. John made it very plain that he was not Elijah.

I want to reemphasize that familiar spirits are very cunning and often quite sophisticated in their operation. Until they begin the phase of maneuvering their victim into the presence of a medium, their operation is extremely difficult to detect without a solid understanding of spiritual matters.

Again, let me state that these familiar spirits are fallen angels[1] which were cast down to the earth thousands of years ago.

Familiar spirits work to possess a human being and make him aware of information they obtained by possessing some other human. In this way a familiar spirit is able to convince his present victim that reincarnation is a reality.

The following story was related to me some years ago by a very dear friend who at the time was a

---

[1]Bible references on fallen angels: 2 Cor. 11:14; 2 Pet. 2:4; Jude 6; Rev. 12:3,4,9.

missionary/evangelist to Africa. Not only did I know the man and his ministry, but we shared a number of mutual acquaintances.

My friend shared with me an occasion of ministry which took him into the African bush country. There he encountered an illiterate, demon-possessed native, who spoke to him in perfect English. For such a thing to happen, some outside force had to be controlling the native.

A demon spoke through the native and said to my friend, "I am of old and I knew the swine."

My friend asked, "Are you telling me that you were among the demons that possessed the maniac of Gadara and were one of those that destroyed the herd of swine?"

The demon answered, "Yes, I am of old, and I know that occasion. I was among them."

By the anointing of the Holy Spirit, the evangelist commanded, "In the name of Jesus, in the same manner that you came out of the maniac of Gadara and set him free, so now shall you loose this man and be gone from him!"

Instantly, the demon loosed his hold and came out. The man was restored and made whole.

In some geographical areas demons have been more free to operate and are more bold than here in the United States. In strong areas of Christianity, they cannot operate so openly, although occasionally such things do happen. Just remember, demons are real. We do have an adversary.

From Leviticus, chapter 20, we read this in verse 27:

A man or woman that hath a familiar spirit, or that is a wizard (or a witch), **shall surely be put to death: they shall stone them with stones: their blood shall be upon them.**

Here is an Old Testament reference which declares that those possessed by familiar spirits will be destroyed. God specifically identifies witches and wizards, the ancient counterparts of our present-day mediums.

Because we are no longer under the Mosaic Law, mediums are not put to death by stoning. However, the sentence of death is not lifted. They will be held responsible for their own death.

Examine the satanic record in the Word of God, and you will see that Satan is a cruel, harsh, brutal task-master. After Satan has captured a person, has used him in every way possible, and has nothing left for him to do, he then maneuvers that person into certain destruction in the most hideous way.

This is true today as people are deceived into a demonic entrapment. Destruction is everywhere. Death by suicide is rampant. The suicide rate among young adults and teenagers is epidemic! Far too often when a suicide is investigated, authorities discover that the victim was involved with either witchcraft or drugs, often both.

God speaks with authority and warns all. He makes it clear that one should not play around with or entertain familiar spirits. Those who become possessed with them are flirting with certain death of a most horrible nature. Leviticus 19:31 instructs us to

regard not them that have familiar spirits, neither seek after wizards, to be defiled by them: I am the Lord your God.

Take note that God gave instruction to His people that they were not to regard those who had familiar spirits; they were not to seek them out.

The practice of consulting fortunetellers and mediums is now more widespread than ever. Clairvoyants and astrologers are in great demand. They claim to have an uncanny ability to offer guidance, advice, or foreknowledge concerning future events in their client's life.

God has clearly forbidden such acts and warns us to disregard those who have familiar spirits. In other words, they are not to be exalted; they are not to be brought in, placed before the public, and given an opportunity to speak.

Too often psychics are invited by university groups, business organizations, civic groups, and even churches, to address their people. Astrologers, clairvoyants, and other mediums should not be brought in like this to pollute the already disturbed minds of literally thousands of people.

That is exactly what God said they would do. He declared that they defile those who hear them. Every astrologer, clairvoyant, wizard, fortuneteller, magician, sorcerer, or medium to which you lend your ears or your eyes for the reading of their materials will defile you. They mislead, misguide, and confuse all upon whom they prey.

Today many of our nation's youth and young adults are having quite an affair with the occult. Occultism and Eastern religions are notorious for spreading witchcraft. Now drug use is greatly increased among them. One must consider the connection between this age group, their practices, and the high murder and suicide rates. Notice also that God clearly declares: **I am the Lord your God**. He indicates that people controlled by familiar spirits attempt to gain complete control of other people.

Can that be true? Do people today view these spiritualists as gods?

Look at the multitudes in the world who follow after these people, becoming hooked on their daily, weekly, and monthly prognostications. People literally worship these astrologers, sorcerers, and clairvoyants.

God says, "I am your God," so let God be God!

Take my word for it: It is exciting to know God and to communicate with Him. He has arranged through Jesus Christ to have a direct audience with anyone who will call on Him in that name. You don't have to go through a medium.

Let's take a look at another passage of scripture that goes along with this one from Leviticus. It is found in the writings of the prophet Isaiah, chapter 8, verse 19:

> **And when they shall say unto you, Seek unto them that have familiar spirits, and unto wizards that peep, and that mutter: should not a people seek unto their God? for the living to the dead?**

Isaiah is simply saying that if there come those who want you to go with them to fortunetellers, magicians, clairvoyants, astrologers, and mediums for consultation, you are about to be trapped. Don't let them talk you into it. Don't go "just for kicks." Don't go whoring after other gods. Don't seek out satanic enchantments and mystic operations.

Turn to the person who extended the invitation and say:

"I have a God Who knows all. He has given me a Textbook in which there is so much blessed information that were I to spend all my life in the research of that Textbook, I'd be extremely informed and blessed. In fact, God is so good that I don't need any other.

"Thank you, but I won't go with you to the fortuneteller (the clairvoyant, the astrologer). I won't go with you to those who are possessed of Satan, whose designs are to defile and capture your mind."

Instead, declare to them that you have a God who is more than enough, a God with whom you are quite pleased. Then offer to take them to your God, through Jesus the Lord!

Christians today are living in the New Testament Church; and New Testament believers have a more direct and personal involvement with God the Father, the Lord Jesus Christ, and the Holy Spirit than did Old Testament saints. There is absolutely no need among the true saints of God for clairvoyants, astrologers, sorcerers, magicians, fortunetellers, and such like.

Jesus is our all in all!

The Word of God is so full of truth, so rich in blessings, and so complete that we don't need anything else.

The operation of the Holy Ghost gives us a sound, healthy, and wholesome spiritual involvement. We don't need to involve ourselves with demonism. We know that Satan is a liar and there is no truth in him. (John 8:44.)

6

Bible Examples
of Familiar Spirits

The Old Testament presents a sterling example of a familiar spirit and its method of operation. This spirit was operating through a witch and working to destroy a man of God — King Saul of Israel.

The story unfolds in First Samuel, chapter 28. I interpret this passage to mean that Saul had quite an experience with familiar spirits.

A study of Saul's life will reveal that he disobeyed God. When he did, the Spirit of the Lord departed from him and a spirit of torment came upon him. Saul's only time of peaceful relaxation was when young David would come before him and play upon his harp. The music served as a tranquilizer for Saul's troubled mind.

As the scene begins, circumstances are going against Saul and Israel. Let's read in chapter 28, beginning with verse 3:

> **Now Samuel was dead, and all Israel had lamented him, and buried him in Ramah, even in his own city. And Saul had put away those that had familiar spirits, and the wizards, out of the land.**

By decree of King Saul, wizards and witches were outlawed and subject to death if they practiced their evil art.

> **The Philistines (Israel's enemy) gathered themselves together, and came and pitched in**

Shunem: and Saul gathered all Israel together, and they pitched in Gilboa.

And when Saul saw the host of the Philistines, he was afraid, and his heart greatly trembled.

And when Saul inquired of the Lord, the Lord answered him not (The Spirit of the Lord had departed from Saul; and God would not carry on a conversation with him.), neither by dreams, nor by Urim, nor by prophets. (Urim was a symbol worn by the priest when seeking the will of God for Israel.)

Then said Saul unto his servants, Seek me a woman that hath a familiar spirit, that I may go to her, and inquire of her. And his servants said to him, Behold, there is a woman that hath a familiar spirit at Endor.

And Saul disguised himself, and put on other raiment, and he went, and two men with him, and they came to the woman by night: and he said, I pray thee, divine unto me by the familiar spirit, and bring me him up, whom I shall name unto thee.

The stage was set! Saul was disobeying God by going to a witch. He and the witch of Endor were about to have a seance and supposedly communicate with the dead.

And the woman said unto him, Behold, thou knowest what Saul hath done, how he hath cut off those that have familiar spirits, and the wizards, out of the land: wherefore then layest thou a snare for my life, to cause me to die?

And Saul sware to her by the Lord saying, As the Lord liveth, there shall not punishment happen to thee for this thing.

Then said the woman, Whom shall I bring up unto thee? And he said, Bring me up Samuel.

> And when the woman saw Samuel, she cried with a loud voice: and the woman spake to Saul, saying, Why hast thou deceived me? for thou art Saul.

> And the king said unto her, Be not afraid: for what sawest thou? And the woman said unto Saul, I saw gods ascending out of the earth.

> And he said unto her, What form is he of? And she said, An old man cometh up; and he is covered with a mantle. And Saul perceived that it was Samuel, and he stooped with his face to the ground, and bowed himself.

Notice it says Saul perceived that it was Samuel. He did not see what the demon-possessed witch saw.

> And Samuel said to Saul, Why hast thou disquieted me, to bring me up? And Saul answered, I am sore distressed; for the Philistines make war against me, and God is departed from me, and answereth me no more, neither by prophets, nor by dreams: therefore I have called thee, that thou mayest make known unto me what I shall do.

> Then said Samuel, Wherefore then dost thou ask of me, seeing the Lord is departed from thee, and is become thine enemy?

> And the Lord hath done to him, as he spake by me: for the Lord hath rent the kingdom out of thine hand, and given it to thy neighbour, even to David: Because thou obeyedst not the voice of the Lord, nor executedst his fierce wrath upon Amalek, therefore hath the Lord done this thing unto thee this day.

We must examine this story closely for there is quite a revelation here. I believe that Saul was so deceived that he actually thought he was conversing with Samuel. However, I interpret it to be a familiar spirit. The woman was totally deceived, and the familiar spirit was using her to deceive Saul.

At this point let me firmly state one fact: The devil has no control over anyone who belongs to God. There is no way Satan could have called Samuel out of Paradise.

Samuel, the godly prophet, was dead; his spirit and soul were in Paradise, a compartment of Sheol[1] (Hebrew word for "the place of the dead"). Sheol is described in the Scriptures as having two great compartments that are separated by an impassable gulf. The Scriptures say it is impossible for anyone to go from one compartment to the other. See Luke 16:19-31.

How then could Satan give this woman the power to call one of God's servants out of Paradise to make an appearance?

She couldn't!

This was not Samuel, the servant of God; I believe it was a familiar spirit which deceived both the witch and Saul. Saul was moved by the description of Samuel that the witch gave. She described him as an old man clothed with a mantle; and her description reminded Saul of Samuel.

---

[1]Sheol, the place of the dead for both the righteous and the wicked, is located in the earth. This we learn from both 1 Sam. 28:11,15 and 1 Pet. 3:19. When Jesus preached to the saints, the area called Paradise — one of the two compartments of Sheol — had not yet been transferred to heaven. Also read Eph. 4:8,9 which states that having descended into the earth, Jesus then ascended and brought all the captives in Paradise with Him, leaving the compartment of Gehenna in the bowels of the earth.

Saul carried on a conversation with a being he assumed to be Samuel; but it was a demon that was literally overpowering Saul's mind. Saul was being totally taken in by Satan's plan.

The demon posing as Samuel knew what had previously taken place.

The Scriptures declare that Satan knows the Word and trembles. How often has he attempted to use the Word of God against you? Don't let him take a scripture verse out of context and misuse it against you.

What a hideous experience involving Saul and familiar spirits! Let me emphasize that Saul was disobeying God by going to this witch. God would not have had any part with this operation, nor would He have allowed His servant Samuel to participate in a demonic scene.

When Saul told the witch that nothing would happen to her, he was lying. God had already spoken through Leviticus 20:27 and proclaimed that she would die.

Whenever you get involved with a spiritualist medium — whether it be an astrologer, clairvoyant, fortuneteller, or a medium at a seance — you lend your mind to Satan's cunning spirits.

Satan will move to capture you in a very cunning way. Then once he has you in the grip of his familiar spirits, it will be hard for you to get free.

Because Saul dealt with witchcraft and familiar spirits, it cost him his life. Let's read First Chronicles 10:13,14:

> So Saul died for his transgression which he committed against the Lord, even against the word of the Lord, which he kept not, and also for asking counsel of one that had a familiar spirit, to inquire of it;

> And inquired not of the Lord: therefore, he slew him, and turned the kingdom unto David the son of Jesse.

Saul paid a big price for delving in witchcraft and familiar spirits: his life!

New Testament Example

In the 16th chapter of Acts, the Apostle Luke is describing an encounter between Paul and a young woman who was possessed with a *spirit of divination*. We read beginning with verse 16:

> And it came to pass, as we went to prayer, a certain damsel possessed with a spirit of divination met us, (Remember, the original Greek says, the spirit of a python) which brought her masters much gain by soothsaying (or by fortunetelling):
> The same followed Paul and us, and cried, saying, These men are the servants of the most high God, which shew unto us the way of salvation.

Notice the shrewd operation of the devil in an attempt to associate his work with God's. It is the same today with all clairvoyants, fortunetellers, astrologers, and mediums. They try to associate their evil work with God.

The scriptural account continues:

And this did she many days. But Paul, being grieved, turned and said to the spirit, I command thee in the name of Jesus Christ to come out of her. And he came out the same hour.

When Paul rebuked the familiar spirit, it released her.

What an event! An entire city was held by Satan through a young woman possessed by a familiar spirit — the spirit of a python. Snakes have a cunning way of charming their intended victims; and once they succeed, the end is tragic. That is what happened to Eve in the Garden of Eden.

A well-known clairvoyant admits to having had the same kind of experience, declaring that she looked into the eyes of a great serpent and beheld the wisdom of the ages. Satan was able to deceive her and convince her that he was of God.

If you read on in Acts, chapter 16, you will find that the men who had used that young woman certainly disliked Paul for what he had done: He had used the power of the name of Jesus to cut off their source of money! They could no longer use the young woman as a source of income.

From ancient times until today, spiritualist mediums of all sorts have used their evil powers to make money. You will find very few, if any, who do not charge for their readings or seances.

7
"Dabbling" in the Occult

Note: Much of the information on witchcraft in this chapter and the next was obtained from books purchased in witchcraft shops — shops which have a "front" such as a regular drugstore but are filled with witchcraft paraphernalia.

Much of my research and many of the stories that I share concerning Satanism come directly from officers in law enforcement agencies in Texas, New York, New Mexico and California and from their confidential case files. My sources are confidential, but I have personally spoken with these officers.

Witchcraft is "1. a) the power or practices of witches; black magic; sorcery. b) An instance of this. 2. bewitching attraction or charm."[1]

"Innocent" Beginnings

"Dabbling" into the occult takes on many, many forms. There have been numerous books written about the occult, especially witchcraft and Satanism. This book cannot even begin to touch the tip of the iceberg on these horrendous subjects, but we have attempted to touch the main points, so that we can better pray for the very survival of our nation!

It begins so "innocently."

---

[1]*Webster's New World Dictionary,* 3rd college ed., s.v. "witchcraft."

All one has to do is to look at the cartoons and many children's television programs on any given Saturday morning. What we remember as the innocence of Mickey Mouse and Donald Duck has given way to many seemingly innocent (some not so "innocent!") shows for our youngsters. Parents don't know what their kids are learning through television. Television now is the number one "babysitter" in the world!

The "innocence" has turned to, literally, little smurfs casting spells on other smurfs. (This show was aired on one particular Saturday.) Our children are bombarded with these kinds of things at very early, vulnerable ages via television.

As our children grow up, we, as parents, tend to lose control of them. We must point part of the finger of blame at ourselves. They have no one to talk to. Many parents simply do not have, or do not take, the time they should in rearing their children, especially in training them in the Word of God. Children are literally dying for our attention! Dear God, help us! From watching certain cartoons, children can move to playing occultic games like Dungeons and Dragons.

I learned of one former witch who related, "I was an honor student in elementary school. As a reward, I played the game Dungeons and Dragons. It's a fantasy, role-playing game that is deadly and deceitful — very occultic.

"Then I progressed to mythology, and ultimately, to hard-core Satanism. But it all started with the game Dungeons and Dragons. The sad part is that I sat under New Age churches which taught me white witchery."

With tears in her eyes, the former witch told of gruesome tales: "Astro-projection is where the spirit body leaves the physical body. I was able to travel to witches' circles, spiritually. I physically witnessed several murders (not when I was involved in astro-projection). I never took my hand to a knife. I witnessed several children who were killed and mutilated. Many were raped before they died. It was horrible!"

Some researchers show that children who watch violent and occultic videos are prime targets for use in witchcraft and Satanism.

Many students in public schools are given a "time of meditation." The students are taught to "relax" and "open their minds." This can give Satan an opportunity to enter their minds if that meditation is not properly channeled through the Holy Spirit.

Yes, the family is disintegrating. Our traditional, moral values are changing before our very eyes.

Satan has done his very best to confuse our society, even many so-called Christians. People are lukewarm in their beliefs and have accepted the lie of Satan that "evil is good...and good is evil."

I shall never forget what the cult leader from Jonestown said to his followers. Jim Jones laughingly spouted off, "What we're doing here is so bizarre, no one will ever believe you." Hundreds of people lost their lives.

Introduction into the occult often begins with parties involving a "good time" with sex and drugs. Then they graduate to learning witchery (Dungeons and Dragons, Ouija boards, white and black magic, and so on). This occurs before one becomes totally involved in Satanism with animal or human sacrifices on an altar. Drugs are used to numb one's system and to call up demons!

Many "innocent" people believe they are dealing with "white magic" — magic which supposedly makes good things happen for people — or the "light side of the Force." Most have no clue that their foundation is already laid for them to worship the devil himself.

No one really thought about witchcraft or Satanism until the end of 1969, when the Charles Manson family killings took place.

The *Los Angeles Times* reported on December 2, 1969, "Police believe they have solved the Sharon Tate murder case and that an occult band of hippies . . . committed the five murders. Members of the band — a mystical, hate-oriented tribe of twentieth century nomads — also are suspected of the LaBianca or 'copy-cat' killings and at least four other comparatively grotesque butcheries. . . ."

The world was shocked. Today, in lesser numbers all at once, these ritualistic slayings occur every day!

This half-nude, drug addicted harem (along with small children) was controlled by an odd, little psychopath named Charles Manson. They obeyed his every command without question. He used constant threats to their lives: "If you ever decide to leave (The Family), I'll take you and hang you upside down, and slit your throat, and use you as an example. . .Follow my orders or meet a horrible death." He kept them mesmerized with terror, drugs, acid-rock music, occult magic, and rampant sex orgies.

Commenting in the early days on the sudden rise of satanic activity, the *Los Angeles Herald-Examiner* reported on December 21, 1969: "Tales of witchcraft cults that sacrifice animals and turn humans into 'slaves of Satan' are coming out of the mountains that form a bucolic backdrop to the Northern California coastal town (of Santa Cruz). Police are paying greater heed to these macabre stories in the aftermath of disclosures about the so-called 'black magic' practices of Charles Manson...."

The report went on, "Investigators also tell of teenagers who described witchcraft initiation ceremonies in which participants must eat the entrails of an animal while its heart is still beating. There are also numerous reports of persons being placed under hypnotic-type spells by a head witch who slips LSD into ceremonial wine...."

Volumes of books have been written about witchcraft over the centuries. There is no doubt that the actual practice of witchcraft is an historical fact of no small political and, of course, spiritual importance.

In addition to the revival of witchcraft and Satanism in the 1960s, I firmly believe that the decade of the sixties will be known as "the decade of decadence."

The 1960s generation was a generation for the most part which had no conscious awareness that there was a God! In 1963 our own Supreme Court took prayer and Bible reading out of our public schools. That devilish seed that was planted by our Supreme Court in 1963 has now grown to be a cancerous sore...one that we, as Americans, cannot escape.

The occult is of the devil. And, friend, the only way out of the occult is through Jesus Christ! God has given to His children power and authority over the devil. (Eph. 6:10-17.) This power is available only through receiving Jesus as Savior and Lord, because Jesus came to destroy the works of the devil, and Jesus is the only Way to God. (1 John 3:8, John 14:6.)

What does God say about our wicked and perverse generation?

> **But it shall come to pass, if you do not obey the voice of thy God, to observe carefully all his commandments and his statutes that I command you today, that all these curses will come on you and overtake you.**
>
> **Deuteronomy 28:15**

Then for the next 53 verses, until the end of that entire chapter, there is a broad listing of curses and plagues.

No Awareness of God

I grew up with a conscious awareness that there was a God. The generation that followed mine grew up with a conscious awareness that there was a God whether the people in that generation were Christians or not. Whether they turned to Jesus or not, they knew there was a God.

They knew that somewhere, sometime, they were going to have to stand before God and give Him an account of their lives. The very knowledge of this, provided a built-in resistance to that which was evil and wrong.

They might have gone ahead and violated that resistance and committed that sin, but nevertheless, they knew that the day would come when they would have to give an answer and be confronted by God Himself.

Our present generation, brought up without prayer and Bible reading in the public schools, does not have a conscious awareness of God. They offer no restraint to evil.

Their openness to witchcraft and Satanism and his wickedness has helped to produce an explosion of corruption that has birthed all manners of troubles and plagues.

But God teaches us to love the sinner and hate the sin. Romans 5:8 teaches us that **while we were yet sinners, Christ died for us.** God gave His only begotten Son for all of us sinners!

People have turned away from reading God's Word. His promises for us can protect us from the wickedness and craftiness of the devil.

Hosea 4:6 says, **My people are destroyed for lack of knowledge.** Ephesians 1:18 encourages us, **The eyes of your understanding being enlightened; that you may know what is the hope of his calling, and what are the riches of the glory of His inheritance in the saints.**

Even secular organizations are becoming aware of the occult powers of Satan. Recent specials, including Geraldo Rivera on television, have increased the awareness of the public. Police organizations are going to "Satanic Seminars" to better prepare them in how to deal with these kinds of people.

The associate editor of our newsletter related to me his story of being in Nigeria at a massive crusade, when over 100 voodoo witch doctors were chanting, trying to put physical hexes on him personally.

I'll never forget interviewing a man who tearfully related his experience with medicine men and the occult. Despite his complete deliverance and that he is now a born-again believer, he remembers his fright "going through that black tunnel" — feeling his body was trapped in a black tunnel with no way out. Tears came to his eyes as he described the experience.

When young children "innocently" begin in the occult, they don't know the severe dangers that soon await them.

Many misguided believers want to "forgive" Satan. They say, "After all, Lucifer was originally given charge over the angels (before the fall). We need to forgive him. Satan is an angel, still to be worshipped."

Dear God! How confused can Christians be? The Scriptures clearly show us that Satan is evil. First Peter 5:8 says: **Be sober, be vigilant; because your adversary the devil, as a roaring lion, walketh about, seeking whom he may devour.**

The list goes on and on, about how we as adults can be "duped" by Satan if we are not grounded in God's Word. Many people watch the re-runs of the "innocent" television show, "Bewitched." A top-seller song was an "innocent" ballad sung by Tom Jones entitled "Daughter of Darkness." We will discuss heavy-metal music in the next chapter.

Witchcraft uses the power of our minds.

A former medicine man admitted, "I learned that I could use my mind to hurt people. Spiritually, I could sacrifice my own family. Once I wanted my teacher to break her leg. She did. I was 'taught' how to injure a person (with my mind). I even demonstrated this for my own mother. Her response: 'My son, you have quite a gift!' There was great joy in getting paid to put spells on people."

A Real Threat

In spite of the proven fact that police know of at least 5,000 satanic groups throughout the United States, many want to "bury their heads in the sand" like an ostrich, pretending these kinds of things simply do not happen, or they are imagined in some disturbed person's mind. When are we going to wake up?

Hocus-pocus. Abracadabra. Surely this is all a fantasy in someone's mind!

Not so.

When driving across the country, in almost every town you can find a palm reader or "advisor." Preceding full-fledged Satanism rituals, there is involvement with witches, palm readers, casting of spells, covens, even witchcraft shops. These are all across the country not just in our "big, bad" metropolis cities — but tucked away in our small, country villages. Witchcraft is everywhere!

Witchcraft Shop

One such witchcraft shop — one with a "front" of a regular drugstore — that was personally visited did multiplied thousands of dollars of business. I guarantee you, pharmaceutical drugs were the farthest thing from someone's mind when he went to that shop!

Witchcraft paraphernalia was everywhere! You name it, this shop (one of thousands in our own United States) had it: candles, incense, birthstones, chuparosa, coffin nails, hex dolls, conjure bags, doll patterns for sorcery, graveyard dirt, herbal baths, hex bags, soaps, medicines, ointments, powders, occult washes, scrubbing compounds, occult "how-to" books, cards, ouija boards, wishing bags, ritual baths, mini-coffins, sorcery doll patterns and so on.

I was appalled! It was like another world! Yet, this is only "minor" compared to the human sacrifices that are happening every day in our own "Christian" country.

Different spells, hexes, unhexing — all the materials that one could use to do witchcraft. My Lord, it was astonishing! One could find "lucky" shark's teeth, horseshoes, "how to conduct seances" books — the works.

What a pitiful feeling came into my stomach. Unfortunately, almost every spell, hex, or witchcraft enchantment has something "Christian" related to it. We learned in our research that these witches study and know all of the Psalms from our Bible. Even in their secret powers and enchantments, they quote actual scripture verses, especially from the precious book of Psalms.

Witchcraft Spells

Witchcraft involves the putting of a "spell" upon other persons or an individual person or thing. In short, a spell manipulates one's mind. In one witchcraft book a spell is described as a ritual which is supposed to have magical powers. A spell is an 'instant miracle,' a way to accomplish objectives without work, study or delay — but the books don't tell of the deadly results!

Many people are drawn by the appeal of this apparently simple solution to their most disturbing problems. Occult authors have invented a spell to solve every possible problem and to attain any imaginable goal, but the methods used are counterfeits of the promises in the Bible. Practicing witchcraft can result only in destruction!

In the name of Jesus Christ, if you are currently under bondage to witchcraft, *flee from it.* May it be a part of you *no more.* Never again! If you are seeking to leave the evils of witchcraft, the end of this book will help you.

Different "spells" in witchcraft, along with certain rituals and use of witchcraft paraphernalia, involve the chanting of certain psalms. For every promise from our Father in the Scriptures, the devil has a counterfeit. Let me say that again: For every miraculous promise that we have from our Father, the devil has a counterfeit! Be alert. Be ready. Study the Scriptures carefully.

I cannot — in my right mind — and with a settled stomach — reveal some of the most degrading, grotesque spells and enchantments that witches use to hex or un-hex people described in some of the books that we used for research on this subject. It was too revolting for me. It was unimaginable.

But, believe me, *the power of Satan is real.* The devilish power of witches is real. Heaven help you if you decide to "dabble" in the occult — if you decide to play with the Ouija board or read and follow the advice of your horoscope.

The devil's goal is for you to burn in hell! Your life will be wretched until you ask God to forgive you and until you seek His deliverance.

Witches even use the Apostles' Creed and the Ten Commandments in their worship. They have changed these; they use what they call the "Devil's Creed."

One of the books we used in research describes the witch's instructions in how to use doll sorcery. The hair cuttings or nail clippings of the person who is the subject of the hex are required to increase the image's talismanic value.

Witchcraft Covens

Ask ten people what witchcraft is and you will receive ten different answers: the world's oldest religion, the practice of black magic, a worldwide secret organization, intercourse with the devil, sorcery with evil intent, devil worship, practitioners of the Black Mass, or the worship of God through the medium of "the Moon Goddess." Their groups are called "covens" and consist of up to thirteen practitioners.

From the moment one becomes interested in any phase of witchcraft, he immediately wants to get involved with a group of witches who will teach him how to perform magical "miracles." However, covens are not searching for many new members, and their membership requirements are very strict. Covens are limited to those who are fully prepared to join in harmony with the particular group.

There are many magazines of an occult nature on newsstands in most cities. Through these public magazines, one may find other "craft" publications to which one can subscribe, magazines not found on public newsracks. These "underground" magazines are published by private organizations. Through these, people grow in witchcraft knowledge by leaps and bounds.

A Serious Situation

You see, it's no longer just an "unlucky 13" or a rabbit's foot. It's no longer a cute, little smurf putting a "spell" on another smurf. It's no longer a game of chance.

The situation is serious. The players are real. The game is eternal life. And Satan is playing "hardball" to win your very soul!

"Dabbling" in the occult is not merely "trying it out." It can cause serious, permanent damage to you, your body, your spirit, and your very soul!

Let God control your life, not yourself! Not Satan. Not magical powers.

I pray that these "innocent beginnings" will never start for anyone reading this book. Flee from this evil! The Bible says, **Resist the devil, and he will flee from you** (James 4:7).

8

Satanism: A Rampaging Obsession

The fatalistic poem below was written by a young student in New Mexico.

> I walk the path of hell, and perish.
> I climb the gate of death, and perish.
> I hear the sound of Satan, and perish.
> I hear the drum of evil, and perish.
> But, I want to die in hell, and perish.
> The world will end, and perish.
> We will all perish with Satan, and die.
> This is all I have to say, I must know. . . .

Satanic worship meeting drawings by this student, found in this youngster's possession, indicated that he had been present at several ritualistic meetings. Yet, he was only a middle school student.

Satanism is the natural follow-up to "innocent" witchcraft. But how many parents know what is really happening in our schools and communities today? Satanism is a rampaging obsession. Too many children know all about the occult and all the various practices that are readily available to them.

Satanism Is Real

Satanism is the "worship of Satan; especially the principles and rites of a cult which travesties Christian ceremonies."[1]

---

[1]Webster's, s.v. "Satanism."

Satanism is horrible and vulgar. It is like a deadly cancer which is quickly eating up the moral fiber of our society. It is spreading like wildfire, with "curiosity and thrill seekers" becoming actual vessels used directly by Satan to spread evil and perverse wickedness with demonic powers, across our land.

It is not my purpose in this book to cover the phenomenal growth of Satanism in America. That would take several books in itself. But I want to hit the main points of what is really happening in our generation. Some of the material in the next few pages might alarm you. So be it. May the Holy Spirit prompt you and challenge you to actual combat of this dreaded obsession in our world.

Some of the stories may be sickening. But let me assure you, I have purposely left out most of my investigation and research so as not to nauseate you with many sickening, grizzly and explicit details that have been documented by law enforcement officials.

Satanism is real. It is not in someone's imagination. The angel of darkness is very much alive and well. The following reports have been declassified for the public to learn about the extent of Satanism in America.

Revealing Case Files

One jailed suspect explained how he became involved in Satanism.

> . . .When I was 15 years old, I seemed to be drawn to something other than Christianity. I thought I would start my own cult. So I started reading things. I read the Bible at first; I couldn't find anything else that I thought was spiritual. Reading the Bible, I

decided that Satan was the good guy and had not been thrown out of heaven, but had come to earth to let people have a good time and do what they wanted to do...I...started calling on Satan to help me...then I saw an ad in a magazine about learning how to be a witch. I started doing the things that it said in the pamphlets and books they sent me.

I did an altar and started saying some of the chants and things that they told me to say. I think the Satanists here got my name from those witch people. They took me to different places. There was a lot of drugs and a lot of sex. I was very interested in that. I was also interested in worshipping Satan. I believed that he was really real.

We went to different houses. Some were very nice. Some, not so nice. Sometimes it was out in the woods. Sometimes it was just me doing things by myself.

Finally those folks asked me if I wanted to become part of their group. I said, "yes." They took me to a cemetery way out in the woods...I had to read several pledges to Satan. I wanted to sign the pledges, but they said, "You can't sign yet. You have to be buried and resurrected first."

They opened one end of the grave and made me crawl in it. They didn't let me have any drugs or anything. They put me in there at midnight and then sealed it up. There was a body in there, but it was nothing more than a skeleton.

There were a few cracks in the top of the grave. I could hear them chanting and dancing around. I was scared. I got kind of cold. Then they poured some kind of liquid on the grave. They may have urinated. It ran down through the cracks and got all over me. That made it worse.

I went all through the next day. They took me at midnight. I was buried for 24 hours. Then my wrists were cut. (Many paragraphs of actual testimony were deleted for the sake of security; also they are too obscene to include in this book)...A lot of people took a drink of my blood. Then I drank the rest of it. I signed the pledges to Satan with my own blood....

There were things that they required us to do...I had to agree to go to a Christian church at least three times a month. They like us to go to a spirit-filled church to show that the power of Satan is stronger than the power of God.[2] You could go there and mock them by being there and make them think that you were one of them...make a mockery of God there.[3]

This teenage boy's testimony continued on and on in detail outlining some of the most vulgar acts I have ever heard about.

Yet he knew about how to study the Bible. That's the shock of this particular account. Dear God, why didn't some parent or some pastor take an interest in this youngster and properly channel his interests into God's Word — instead of letting him pervert God's Holy Word?

Many documented police investigations have indicated that many witch covens have a plan of infiltrating churches. Some witches have been literally caught at the back of the church, casting spells on pastors as they preached their Sunday morning sermons!

Many abused children are prime targets for Satanic cults. We watched the news in shock as the McMartin

---

[2]This opinion, of course, is erroneous.

[3]This account and the others in this chapter marked with an asterisk (*) are from the case files of Lyle J. Rapacki, Consultant of Occult-Related Crimes and Deviant Movements, P.O. Box 42, Flagstaff, Arizona 86002. Used by permission.

Pre-School molestation case became public in the fall of 1983 in Los Angeles, California. Scores of children have been molested. But child abuse continues on a daily basis here in the United States. Much of that, documented by authorities who are willing to share, is via satanic worship.

An Unwilling Participant

The following story is vivid in detail. Please skip to the heading "The Only Way To Get Out of Satanism" if you feel you do not want to read it or the other accounts following it.

The testimony is from a girl in California who was a witness to and unwilling participant in a human sacrifice ritual ceremony. It is from a police file — an eye witness account related to police in an investigation.

I think my father was trying to gain satanic power. I remember going with my father to a man's apartment. He wanted to buy a woman. The man wanted to exchange the woman for me. I was a 7-year-old kid at the time.

Later, when she came into the room, they made her take her clothes off and lie on the table. There were men and women in the room. . .she looked at me, and I couldn't save her. They had sex with her before and after she was dead. They made me lie on top of her when she was dead!

They had a stainless steel trough under the table to catch the blood. My mother held my arms and made me cut the woman's wrists with a razor blade. The dying lady looked at me as I was doing it, as if she couldn't believe what was happening. I don't think she could believe she was being killed by a little girl.

Her gruesome testimony continues:

> I lost my virginity in the Bride of Satan ceremony. It was the usual coven (of witches). It was nighttime. My father was standing at the altar. I walked to the altar alone. The people chanted, "Hail, Bride of Satan. Welcome, Bride of Satan to our midst."
>
> I was crying. They were greeting me with clenched fists. They told me to kneel on the table (altar) in front of my father. They all walked around the altar twice and touched the top of my head. They told me to lie down on my back on the altar. Then they took turns doing what they did last night....*

Tragic. Sickening. Deplorable.

There is no happy ending to this story. It has not been told to frighten you, but to cause you to understand that the true born-again Church is the *only* group of people on the earth who can do anything about this problem.

The Body of Christ has forgotten about the power of prayer. In this sense, the Church has been promiscuous since the fifties. Christians need to fast and pray concerning this and learn the power of prayer — of the Word, of the Holy Spirit, of the name of Jesus. Satan is no match for this action.

My friend, these kinds of experiences are happening in our country on a regular basis. As Christians, we need to wake up to the real world. We must put on the whole armor of God so we can do literal battle with Satan. I didn't want to scare or nauseate you, but I wanted to share some "real-life" scenarios, verified by police investigations, so you could be aware of the enormity of the problem.

Documented statistics from different volumes show exactly how widespread this epidemic is. There are more than 5,000 satanic groups in the United States as I mentioned previously. Sometimes it is the lack of knowledge which causes people to fear Satan. Remember, Hosea 4:6 says, **My people are destroyed for lack of knowledge.**

More Murder

Permit me to share one more police testimony about a teenaged boy who played Dungeons and Dragons and was given a prayer to Satan by a witch.

When he was alone one night, he repeated that prayer. He felt a demonic presence and saw demons flying. In school he wrote a lengthy essay in which he said, "I love my friends. I love my family. But I am free. I can kill without remorse and I feel no regret or sorrow. . . ."

Later he shot and killed a convenience store clerk who earlier had earlier refused to sell him beer. Then a few months later, he slipped quietly into his parents' bedroom and shot them each through the head while they slept.*

In a nearby state a couple of years ago, a 14-year-old boy approached a total stranger and slit the stranger's throat from ear to ear. Perplexed officers, searching for a motive, didn't understand. But the officer said to me, "It all started adding up, when I realized that the perpetrator walked back and forth through the pool of blood." The boy later said, "I didn't do it. Someone else did it. It was the devil!"

Another police officer revealed to me a real tragedy, "The kids already know about Satanism. We're just providing preventive measures."

The Only Way
To Get Out of Satanism

"The only way to get out of Satanism is through Jesus Christ!" An ex-witch, now a born again Christian, made that statement. How true that is. That's why you and I need to be on our knees constantly. Amen. Jesus Christ is the only answer.

Three Groups of Satanists

There are three basic groups of Satanists:

1. Self-stylers. Those who "dabble" in the occult. They play the game of Dungeons and Dragons, play with the Ouija board, read the daily horoscope and so on.

2. Religious Satanists. Those who publicly confess their allegiance to Satan.

3. Cult Satanists. These are more clandestine; and deal with some illegal activities, including animal and human sacrifices.

Satanism expert Arthur Lyons (author of the book, *The Second Coming: Satanism in America*) claims that "the United States has the fastest growing and most highly developed body of Satanists in the world."

Policemen tell me of many of their investigations. One policeman explained to me that in order for someone to be initiated into Satanism, he must go through such rituals as saying a Satanic prayer and promising that he will sacrifice babies.

He told me, "Satanists believe the younger the victim, the more innocent. The more innocent, the more precious to God. The more precious to God, the more the defilement."

"Satanists sacrifice animals because they want to gain that animal's power. Many dogs are sacrificed, because dog spelled backwards is 'god.' "

"Satanists believe that when they commit suicide, they will be reincarnated and come back with more power."

They believe that anything goes!

Satanism provides gratification of the flesh, gratification of the ego, and most importantly — power.

Many children are reported missing every year. A number, of course, are runaways. However, some authorities believe that some children are part of occultic practices of human sacrifices. Children are the most sought after commodities. One particular satanic sect is "required to kill 12 people a year in order to advance to a 'higher level.' "

Although I believe this next figure is too high and may be exaggerated and hard to prove, Dr. Al Carlisle of the Utah State Prison System has estimated *"between forty and sixty thousand human beings are killed through satanic ritual homicides in the United States each year!"* Alarmingly, that gives us something to think about.

Another law enforcement official, not wanting to be named, admitted to me, "We have evidence that some girls are getting pregnant for sacrifice purposes."

The ex-witch who had witnessed children being mutilated and murdered reported, "I remember the screams. There are 'breeding farms' where they breed babies for occult activities and sacrifices. Innocent, runaway teenagers are taken to farms. The girls that are taken are beautiful, pretty and innocent. They must be virgins. There are 'recruiters' in the schools."

She went on to tearfully relate, "One night I asked Satan to come into my heart. It was very painful when he entered. I remember falling to the floor. I would call up demons and curse people. A funny thing: if the people were Christians, the demons could not harm them. The occult is everywhere!"

Law Enforcement Is Trying

There are many law enforcement task forces which deal specifically with Satanism. The Cult Awareness Network has offices in nearly 40 states. The C.C.I.N. (Cult Crime Impact Network) is a national organization of police officers which deals in investigating the occult.

Lt. Larry Jones is president of the board of directors for the C.C.I.N., which attempts to track underground Satanism and educate law enforcement officers about occult crimes. Some occult-related crimes are never seen as satanic, simply because the police don't know what they are looking for.

Jones states, "Since Satanists mix religion and crime, we may have to mix religion and law enforcement to catch them."

However, it is not illegal to be a Satanist. They are protected under the First Amendment of the United States Constitution.

One lieutenant confided to me, "It is very hard to investigate this type of crime. Very rarely are these people brought to justice."

Another policeman declared, "Just as you have the right to be a Christian, they have the right to be a Satanist. In fact, in our depositions, we can no longer say the word, 'Satanism.' We cannot offend them. Our laws protect all religious groups including Satanists."

The Church of Satan

Anton LaVey is America's leading Satanist, "pastoring" the tax-exempt Church of Satan in San Francisco, California. In 1970, when LaVey's group was less than five years old, he claimed 7,000 members. That figure is too overwhelming for us to comprehend. He appeared in the movie, *Rosemary's Baby*, as the personification of the devil. He has written three best-selling books to introduce Satan to the world, including *The Satanic Bible, The Complete Witch,* and *Satanic Rituals.*

Since *The Satanic Bible* was first published in December 1969, it has sold over 700,000 copies!

LaVey's Church has a code of precepts called "the nine Satanic statements":

1) Satan represents indulgence, instead of abstinence.

2) Satan represents vital existence, instead of spiritual dreams.

3) Satan represents undefiled wisdom, instead of hypocritical self-deceit.

4) Satan represents kindness to those who deserve it, instead of love wasted on ingrates.

5) Satan represents vengeance, instead of turning the other cheek.

6) Satan represents responsibility to the responsible, instead of concern for psychic vampires.

7) Satan represents man as just another animal, sometimes better, more often worse than those that walk on all fours, who because of his "divine spiritual and intellectual development," has become the most vicious animal of them all.

8) Satan represents all of the so-called sins as they all lead to physical, mental, or emotional gratification.

9) Satan has been the best friend the Church has ever had, as he has kept it in business all these years.

Possible Terrorism

Concerned citizens and Christians realize that under the influence of Satan, anyone possessed could do just about anything: even blow up a plane, just like a terrorist.

One spokesman for a satanic group commented, "Satan is demanding more and more sacrifices."

Satanism is the ultimate justification for terrorism. For someone who feels that he is under Satan's influence, the destruction of an airliner full of people is justifiable if Satan demands it.

Satanism is becoming the "religion of choice" by many violent, racist, right-wing youth gangs.

Many of the alienated white working class youths who drift into Satanism and eventually into neo-Nazi groups share one common trait with youthful terrorists the world over: a tremendous feeling of powerlessness, the feeling that they are no longer in control of their lives and their destiny.

One youthful "skinhead," who had Satanist and Nazi tattoos all over his body, remarked to a prison psychiatrist, "Hey, Christ and Satan have been slugging it around for thousands of years. Look around you, man. Look at the world. Who do you think is winning? I'm gonna stick with the winner."

Many historians point out that Adolph Hitler and many high-ranking officers of the Third Reich were heavily involved in Satanism.

Heavy Metal Music

There is no need to point out that Satanism is overtly ingrained into heavy metal music. Many books have exposed the satanic influence in today's heavy metal or black metal music.

Beggars Banquet was a top-selling album for the rock-and-roll favorite group, The Rolling Stones. It includes a song called "Symphony for the Devil."

Punk album, "I Kill Children," by the group, The Dead Kennedys, has unthinkable words about enjoying destroying children. What in this world is happening to our youth? With words like the ones in that song, how can we help?

What can one say to the ex-witch who admits, "Heavy metal music engulfed my life. It hypnotized me"?

Witchcraft, Satanism, familiar spirits — it's all a deadly game. Dabbling in these occultic practices is a road that leads straight to hell!

When will America wake up?

When will Christians recognize the severe problems that are happening as a result of demonic activity?

Dear God, *I pray it is soon!*

9

Witchcraft and Familiar Spirits — What You Can Do About It

This book is by no means an exhaustive study of witchcraft or the operation of familiar spirits. In fact, there is even more evidence within the Scriptures, but to share it would be somewhat repetitious.

The main point is that we be well informed. That puts us at an advantage over our adversary, the devil, and his operation.

If a believer stays filled with the Holy Spirit and studies the Bible, it isn't likely he will ever have a problem with a familiar spirit. The person who is sensitive to the Holy Spirit and abides in the Word will also have the ability to discern spirit operation.

However, the unsaved person and the one who is without true spiritual life has little or no protection from the cunning, deceitful work of familiar spirits, which accounts for the fact that an estimated 160 million Americans today are involved in some form of witchcraft. (This is a conservative estimate from various sources. Numbers also run up to 200 million.)

The question is often asked: How does a person know if a familiar spirit is working on him?

The answer comes in two parts:

First, if you are a spiritual person, the Holy Spirit will help you detect a familiar spirit through the gift of discerning of spirits. (1 Cor. 12:10.)

Second, if you are not spiritually inclined, the very moment you begin to realize that certain forms of witchcraft (horoscope, Ouija boards, fortunetellers, astrology) are becoming interesting and attractive to you, look out! You can be sure that a familiar spirit has been at work, creating his detailed file on your life. He will then begin his maneuvering to get you into the presence of a demon-controlled spiritualist medium.

When you recognize that activity, it is time to call on God through Jesus to break the hold and influence of that familiar spirit. Seek out a godly person who can pray with you and get you into the Word of God.

Don't play games with forms of witchcraft. It is a deadly involvement!

Don't do things just for kicks. Remember, it is forbidden by the Scriptures to participate in these activities.

Allow no one, regardless of how intelligent he may seem, to get you involved with witchcraft or drugs.

One of the oldest tricks is the attempt to draw another person into the scene by claiming it to be a great way to "expand the mind." Through drugs and witchcraft, the mind is controlled, not expanded.

Satan is constantly at work to control a person's mind. Drugs and witchcraft open the mind to strong satanic influence and eventual possession.

If this book has caused you to recognize Satan's operation in your life and his attempt to capture you, this is the moment to break off the act. Call on the Lord Jesus and be free of Satan's snare.

To stay free of any such entrapment, take Jesus as your Savior and begin to feed your spirit and your soul on the exciting Word of God.

The Apostle Paul teaches us to be spiritually minded. In Romans 8:5,6 he wrote:

> **For they that are after the flesh do mind the things of the flesh; but they that are after the Spirit the things of the Spirit.**
>
> **For to be carnally minded is death; but to be spiritually minded is life and peace.**

The prophet Isaiah declares of God:

> **Thou wilt keep him in perfect peace, whose mind is stayed on thee: because he trusteth in thee.**
>
> **Isaiah 26:3**

One final word concerning the signs of the zodiac: A thorough research into church history reveals no evidence of the use of such signs by any of the Bible-believing followers of Jesus Christ.

Let it be known: Our birth sign is the cross of Jesus, not some pagan sign!

Both Jesus and the Apostle John tell the Christian that he has passed from death to life. (See John 5:24; 1 John 3:14.) The cross is our birth sign. Read carefully Ephesians 2:1-7. It is a real eye-opener!

Should you have any jewelry, clothing, or other items displaying signs of the zodiac, destroy them immediately! Melt down the jewelry and give it to some worthy outreach to win souls to the Lord Jesus Christ.

Read Acts 19:18-20 and notice the action taken by believers after Paul had taught them the truth. When they were completely rid of all their books and evil paraphernalia, it says the Word of God grew mightily among them and prevailed!

Don't allow involvement with any form of witchcraft to prevent your spiritual growth.

Rid yourself and your dwelling place of all materials dealing with witchcraft in any form. Don't give them away or put them in the garbage — destroy them!

Remember, don't be deceived by thinking that mediums and the type of paraphernalia we are discussing in this book are of God. This is what Satan wants you to believe. God's Word reveals them to be liars.

I pray that the information in this book will be not only an aid to you, but that you will use it to aid others. The opposite of dealing in witchcraft and familiar spirits is coming into the abundant life of Christ and staying filled with the Holy Spirit of God.

Receive Your Freedom

If you are now, or even have been, involved in any form of witchcraft — no matter how elementary it may seem — you need to renounce it in Jesus' name.

You may have thought that reading the daily horoscope, playing with a Ouija board, or visiting the fortuneteller at a carnival was harmless and a fun thing to do, but God's Word says it is forbidden. (See Scripture references later in this chapter.) Satan wants to destroy your life, and he will do whatever he can any way he can, to accomplish this.

If any of the various forms of witchcraft are becoming more and more appealing to you, then you can be sure that a familiar spirit has taken an assignment against you.

As God's child, saved and filled with the Holy Spirit, you are not immune to Satan's working against you. He will try his best to ensnare you, but one thing you can be sure of: as a born-again believer, you have been given authority over Satan. By the power in the name of Jesus, you can be free of satanic influence over your life the moment you detect it.

You can pray a prayer of freedom from oppression now. Simply speak this prayer aloud to your heavenly Father from the sincerity of your heart:

Father, I come to You in the name of Jesus. Your Word says that witchcraft in any form is an abomination to You. I renounce witchcraft and ask Your forgiveness for participating in _____ (renounce by name, using the list which follows this prayer).

In Jesus' name and by His authority, I break the power of any familiar spirit that has been assigned against me. Satan, you will no longer have a hold over me or influence my life!

Now, Father, I thank You for Your forgiveness. I receive by faith my complete deliverance and total freedom, in Jesus' name.

If the Son therefore shall make you free, ye shall be free indeed.

John 8:36

Forms of Witchcraft

Astrology	Necromancy
Card-reading	Numerology
Crystal ball-gazing	Ouija Boards
Cult & Occult Practices	Out-of-Body Travel
Extrasensory Perception (ESP)	Palmistry
Fire-gazing	Pendulum
Fortunetelling	Phrenology
Handwriting Analysis	Seances
Horoscopes	Spiritualism
Hypnotism	Table-tipping
Idol Worship	Theosophy
Magic	Voodoo
Mediums	Water-divining
Metaphysics	Witchcraft

Scriptures on Witchcraft and Familiar Spirits

Take ye therefore good heed unto yourselves...

And lest thou lift up thine eyes unto heaven, and when thou seest the sun, and the moon, and the stars, even all the host of heaven, shouldest be driven to worship them, and serve them, which the Lord thy God hath divided unto all nations under the whole heaven.

Deuteronomy 4:15,19

And God spake all these words, saying,

I am the Lord thy God, which have brought thee out of the land of Egypt, out of the house of bondage.

Thou shalt have no other gods before me.

Thou shalt not make unto thee any graven image, or any likeness of any thing that is in heaven above (planets and stars), or that is in the earth beneath, or that is in the water under the earth:

Thou shalt not bow down thyself to them, nor serve them: for I the Lord thy God am a jealous God, visiting the iniquity of the fathers upon the children unto the third and fourth generation of them that hate me;

And shewing mercy unto thousands of them that love me, and keep my commandments.

Exodus 20:1-6

There shall not be found among you any one who makes his son or daughter pass through the fire, or who uses divination, or is a soothsayer, or an augur, or a sorcerer,

Or a charmer, or a medium, or a wizard, or a necromancer.

For all who do these things are an abomination to the Lord.

Deuteronomy 18:10-12 AMP

Turn not to those [mediums] who have familiar spirits, or to wizards; do not seek them out to be defiled by them. I am the Lord your God.

Leviticus 19:31 AMP

The person who turns to those who have familiar spirits and to wizards, [being unfaithful to Israel's Maker Who is her Husband, and thus] playing the harlot after them, I will set My face against that person and will cut him off from among his people [that he may not be included in the atonement made for them]...

A man or woman who is a medium and has a familiar spirit or is a wizard, shall surely be put to death, be stoned with stones; their blood shall be upon them.

Leviticus 20:6,27 AMP

Moreover, Josiah put away the mediums, the wizards, the teraphim [household gods], the idols and

89

all the abominations that were seen in Judah and in Jerusalem, that he might establish the words of the law written in the book found by Hilkiah the priest in the house of the Lord.

2 Kings 23:24 AMP

So Saul died for his trespass against the Lord [in sparing Amalek], for his unfaithfulness in not keeping God's word, and also for consulting [a medium with] a spirit of the dead, to inquire pleadingly of it.

1 Chronicles 10:13 AMP

And he (Manasseh) burned his children as an offering [to his god] in the valley of the son of Hinnom, and practiced soothsaying, augury, and sorcery, and dealt with mediums and wizards. He did much evil in the sight of the Lord, provoking Him to anger.

2 Chronicles 33:6 AMP

And when the people [instead of putting their trust in God] shall say to you, Consult for direction mediums and wizards who chirp and mutter, should not a people seek and consult their God? Should they consult the dead on behalf of the living?

Isaiah 8:19 AMP

He who is victorious shall inherit all these things, and I will be a God to him and he shall be My Son.

. . . as for murderers and the lewd and adulterous and the practicers of magic arts and the idolaters [those who give supreme devotion to any one or anything other than God] and all liars [those who knowingly convey untruth by word or deed, all of these shall have] their part in the lake that blazes with fire and brimstone. This is the second death.

Revelation 21:7,8 AMP

Scriptures on Devil Worship

The Old Testament provides us with numerous references to demon or devil worship. We know the practice was widespread among the people who did not know the God of Israel. The Biblical record reveals the sacrifice of sons and daughters; in other words, human sacrifice. How utterly tragic; and yet worse is the fact that the children of Israel did likewise. When one's heart is turned away from God and Satan discovers the empty soul, he moves in.

Jesus taught:

> When the unclean spirit is gone out of a man, he walketh through dry places, seeking rest, and findeth none.
>
> Then he saith, I will return into my house from whence I came out; and when he is come, he findeth it empty, swept, and garnished.
>
> Then goeth he, and taketh with himself seven other spirits more wicked than himself, and they enter and dwell there: and the last state of that man is worse than the first. Even so shall it be also with this wicked generation.
>
> **Matthew 12:43**

Below are Old and New Testament references worthy of serious consideration:

> And they shall no more offer their sacrifices unto devils, after whom they have gone a whoring. This shall be a statute for ever unto them throughout their generations.
>
> **Leviticus 17:7**
>
> They sacrificed unto devils, not to God; to gods whom they knew not, to new gods that came newly up, whom your fathers feared not.
>
> **Deuteronomy 32:17**

Yea, they sacrificed their sons and their daughters unto devils,

And shed innocent blood, even the blood of their sons and of their daughters, whom they sacrificed unto the idols of Canaan: and the land was polluted with blood.

Psalm 106:37,38

But I say, that the things which the Gentiles sacrifice, they sacrifice to devils, and not to God: and I would not that ye should have fellowship with devils.

1 Corinthians 10:20

And the rest of the men which were not killed by these plagues yet repented not of the works of their hands, that they should not worship devils, and idols of gold, and silver, and brass, and stone, and of wood: which neither can see, nor hear, nor walk.

Neither repented they of their murders, nor of their sorceries, nor of their fornication, nor of their thefts.

Revelation 9:20,21

The verses that stand out are Revelation 9:20,21. The setting for this verse is shortly after mid-Tribulation, when God is releasing plagues and wrath upon the ungodly. Standing out is the fact that demons will be worshipped, while murder, sorcery, sexual immorality and theft prevail.

The word *sorcery* as used in this reference means, "enchantments with drugs."

Both enchantments and drugs are used to control one's mind. This certainly accounts for increased satanic worship and human sacrifice, which of course, is murder.

The satanic worship and human sacrifices now evident worldwide are forerunners of things to come. In other words, it will get worse as we approach the period identified as the Tribulation.

Haven't you noticed we are running out of the middle of the road! The once prominent gray area is almost gone!

With the decade of the fifties, polarization definitely began. One will soon be either on God's side or the devil's side. No middle of the road or gray area.

What a challenge to those of us who know Jesus as our Savior. If ever the stage was set for the Body of Christ (the true Church) to come front and center, this is the time.

We must obey the commands and the Word of God! When we do so, Satan is powerless before us! James 4:7 says, **Submit yourselves therefore to God. Resist the devil, and he will flee from you.**

God has prepared us for this very hour. So be strong in the Lord and the power of his might. Put on the whole armor of God, that you may be able to stand against the wiles of the devil. (Eph. 6:10,11).

For though we walk in the flesh, we do not war according to the flesh:

For the weapons of our warfare are not carnal, but mighty through God to the pulling down of strong holds;

Casting down imaginations, and every high thing that exalteth itself against the knowledge of God, and bringing into captivity every thought to the obedience of Christ.

2 Corinthians 10:3-6

Never forget the mind is the battlefield. Satan is the arch deceiver; therefore, he is constantly attempting to gain control over one's mind. He is a master at brainwashing; however, as long as one is in Christ Jesus, he/she has the mind of Christ. It is impossible for Satan to compete with the mind of Christ. Furthermore, the believer wears God's armor, uses his weapons, and is covered with the blood of the lamb. The born-again believer should also know that he has enlisted in God's army and should conduct himself as a soldier. (See 2 Tim. 2:3,4.)

Since we are in warfare, it is vital that the believer be filled with the Holy Spirit. I am referring to the experience made available to the believer in Acts 2. To have the power, energy and the ability of God, you must be baptized in the Holy Spirit. In this case, Jesus is the baptizer. (Matt. 3:11.) Surely no one is fearful of receiving from the hands of Jesus.

The receiving of the Holy Spirit also provides the Holy Spirit-filled believers with the ability to communicate with God in heavenly languages. (See Acts 2:4,1; Cor. 14:2,4). These verses establish this ability and show its benefits. Every believer ought to desire to talk to God and know that Satan can't translate the message.

All the above is simply declaring that the believer does not fear Satan or Satanism. Therefore, we are able to lovingly minister to those who have been ensnared. The only hope for those caught in the web of Satanism is the love of God, Who gave His Son Jesus for them.

We must be ready to minister to these tormented people.

Minister with much love and unswerving patience. Learn to listen and let them tell their story. Be prepared to hear a vile, vulgar, brutal and tormented story. Don't attempt to force the Word down their throats. Remember, they have been in intense bondage and you don't want them to feel they are exchanging one bondage for another. They need love, understanding, a covering and patience. Realize that their satanic crowd doesn't want to give them up and may even come to take them back. So you must provide protection when necessary.

Remember, **greater is he that is in you, than he that is in the world** (1 John 4:4). Satan is our defeated foe and God has equipped us to keep him defeated. We are more than conquerors through Jesus Christ, so let's live, act and minister that truth.

A Word to the One Held by Satan

Having read this book and the scriptures in the Bible, I pray you are now more enlightened. I'm certain that the powerful Word of God has broken Satan's control over your mind. That control will remain broken if you will follow these steps:

1. Ask Jesus to come into your heart. Pray this simple prayer: "Jesus, I believe You are the Son of God. I ask You now to come into my heart; wash me with Your blood, and I will be clean. Now I thank You for hearing my prayer. I believe I am saved, born again. In Your name, Jesus, Satan's power is now broken from my life and I thank You. Romans 10:9,10 says, **If thou shalt confess with thy mouth the Lord Jesus, and shalt believe in thine heart that God hath raised him from**

the dead, thou shalt be saved. **For with the heart man believeth unto righteousness; and with the mouth confession is made unto salvation.**

2. Begin to say, "Jesus is my Savior." Say it again and again.

3. Renounce Satan and all Satanism, in the name of Jesus. Jesus said, **And whatsoever ye shall ask in my name, that will I do, that the Father may be glorified in the Son** (John 14:13). **In my name shall they cast out devils...** (Mark 16:17).

4. Locate some born again, Holy Spirit-filled Christians, and ask them to pray with you and help you.

5. If you don't have a Bible, ask for one or buy one.

6. In a quiet time, read the book of St. John to yourself — aloud!

7. Ask the believers to pray and believe with you to receive the baptism of the Holy Spirit.

8. Be patient with yourself and with those praying with you and teaching you.

9. Stay with the believers who lift up Jesus and show you love.

10. Remember, now that Jesus has come into your heart and life, First John 4:4 declares, **Ye are of God, little children, and have overcome them: because greater is he** (Jesus) **that is in you, than he** (Satan) **that is in the world.**

I believe in you and Jesus. Together, Satan is no match for you. However, we start out as babes in Christ.

Grow up in Christ before you start trying to defeat Satan all by yourself.

To receive Hilton Sutton's
monthly publication, *Update*, write:

Mission To America
736 Wilson Road
Humble, Texas 77338

*Please include your prayer requests
and comments when you write.*

Bibliography

Books

Johnston, Jerry. *The Edge of Evil: The Rise of Satanism in North America.* Texas: Word Publishers, 1989.

Riva, Anna. *The Modern Witchcraft Spellbook.* California: International Imports, 1988 reprint.

Riva, Anna. *Spellcraft, Hexcraft, and Witchcraft.* California: International Imports, 1977.

Stratford, Lauren. *Satan's Underground.* Oregon: Harvest House Publishers, 1988.

Articles

Armstrong, Bob. "Satanism Seminar Alerts Many to Dangers!" *Navajo Neighbors,* summer 1989.

Lilley, Jeff. "Evil in the Land." *Moody Monthly,* March 1989.

"SATANISM: A Practical Guide to Witch Hunting." *American Opinion* Magazine. September 1970.

Yaeger, Carl H., "Satanism and Terrorism." *American Survival Guide.* April 1989, pp. 44-46.

Video

"America's Best Kept Secret (Satanism)." *Passport* Magazine Production.

Hilton Sutton is regarded by many as the nation's foremost authority on Bible prophecy as related to current events and world affairs.

As an ordained minister of the Gospel, Dr. Sutton served as pastor for several years before being directed by the Holy Spirit into the evangelistic field. Today he travels throughout the world, teaching and preaching the Word. He takes the words of the most accurate news report ever — the Word of God — and relates it to the news today.

Having spent over twenty-five years researching and studying the book of Revelation, Hilton Sutton explains Bible prophecy and world affairs to the people in a way that is clear, concise, and easy to understand. He presents his messages on a layman's level and shows the Bible to be the most accurate, up-to-date book ever written.

Dr. Sutton and his family make their home in Humble, Texas, where he serves as chairman of the board of Mission To America, a Christian organization dedicated to carrying the Gospel of Jesus Christ to the world.

Books by Hilton Sutton

Revelation — God's Grand Finale

*The Pre-Tribulation Rapture
of the Church*

U.S. in Prophetic Events

**Available at your local
bookstore or by writing:**

HARRISON HOUSE
P. O. Box 35035
Tulsa, OK 74153